Self-Preservation: Cultivating Your Mindset

A Guide to a Limitless Journey

Adrian Horstead

Formatting by **Ashley Jane Aesthetics**
Cover Art: **A. Shea Artistry**

SELF-PRESERVATION/Adrian Horstead
1st edition
ISBN: 979-8-234-09876-4

First and foremost, I want to thank The Most High for allowing me the time and resources to write this book. Thank you, Mom, Pops, and Broham for being the glue that holds my life together.

I want to dedicate this book to my late cousin Amos Matthews. Thank you, cuzzo for always believing in me and inspiring me to be steadfast and stand on business.

Preface

What do you demand of your life?
What is God's purpose for your life?

Align what you demand of your life along with what God demands of your life, and your life will be filled with lessons and blessings.

Have you ever accepted Jesus Christ into your life?
If you have not, say this prayer:

Lord, I ask you to take over my life and guide me. Lord, thank you for sending Your Son to die for my sins, and I accept this life in oneness with You. Now, God show me to the truth and light.

Through Jesus Christ, you are gifted with everlasting life.

DAY 1
Discipleship and Mentorship

While in college, I had the opportunity to be a part of a discipleship group. You may ask, what is a discipleship? Discipleship involves meeting with like-minded individuals for personal ongoing life journeys of faith and relationships. It also is the practice of mentoring others to trust and follow Him. We met once a week for 2-3 hours. During the discipleship we prayed, worshipped, and spoke about our relationship with God. We also read books that aligned with spreading the Gospel. While forming bonds with kindred spirits, you must not forget that God is the reason. Always be honest with yourself and allow your tongue to be an overflow of your mind.

Matthew 28:18-20: "Then Jesus came to them and said, "All authority in heaven and on earth has been given to me. Therefore, go and make disciples of all nations, baptizing them in the name of the Father and of the Son and of the Holy Spirit, and teaching them to obey everything I have commanded you. And surely, I am with you always to the very end of age."

"A mentor is someone who sees more talent and ability within you, than you see in yourself, and helps bring it out."

- Bob Proctor

To Do: I challenge you while reading this book to form a **discipleship** group with one or more people.

Notes:

DAY 2
Trauma

Understanding what **trauma** is can be key to releasing any strongholds that may be attached to these traumas. **Trauma** is a very convincing emotional response to an action or event that drowns our ability to cope. One **trauma** that mom and I joke about is hoarding. My mom says that she collects clothes and shoes simply because she lacked adequate clothes and shoes when she was growing up.

It is extremely beneficial to speak to a trusted individual about our **traumas**. I challenge you while speaking about these **traumas** to ask God to release any strongholds attached to these **traumas**. Pray for specifics with extreme clarity.

Psalms 46:1-3: "For the director of music.

Of the Sons of Korah, According to Alamath. A song.

God is our refuge and strength,

An ever-present help in trouble.

There will not be fear, though the earth

Give way and the mountains fall

Into the heart of the sea.

Though its waters roar and foam and

The mountains quake with their singing.

"Trauma fractures comprehension as a pebble shatters a windshield."

- Jane Leavy

Notes:

DAY 3
Accountability

Accountability is the brother to integrity and discipline. Accountability plus integrity and discipline equates to a limitless journey in life. Condition yourself to take responsibility for the good and bad aspects of your life. You cannot grow without feedback and **accountability**. Apostle Paul said it best in Romans Chapter 14 verse 12.

Romans 14:12- "So then, each of us will give an account of ourselves to God."

"The whole purpose of education is to turn mirrors into windows."

- Sydney J. Harris

To Do: For the next 14 days, I want you to rewire your mind. Every day for the next 14 days write down three things for which you are grateful.

Notes:

DAY 4
Integrity

You must maintain **integrity** throughout each day. Doing the morally right thing, regardless of your circumstances, gives you the character needed for a limitless life journey. Not allowing your character to be compromised also keeps your moral compass calibrated. The average camper knows that your compass must be calibrated to keep its true north position. Self-determination is the need to act on and control one's environment. God commands us to take up His cross daily. This prepares you for the situations in life that can compromise your character. When variations occur in your life, it usually causes your moral compass to lose its true north position. You must be consistent and not deviate.

Proverbs 10:9: "Whoever walks in integrity walks securely, but whoever takes crooked paths will be found out."

"Success is to be measured not so much by the position that one has reached in life as by the obstacles which he has overcome."

- Booker T. Washington

Notes:

DAY 5
Discipline

Accountability, integrity, discipline. **Discipline** is the greatest of the three. With discipline, you can have limitless days. Training your mind to create a tailored curriculum gives infinite freedom. Your DNA is specifically designed for you. **Discipline** is the keystone that is built with accountability and integrity. New behavior replaces ineffective habits!

Luke 9:23-24: "Whoever wants to be my disciple must deny themselves and take up their cross daily and follow me. For whoever wants to save their life will lose it, but whoever loses their life for me will save it."

"Small disciplines repeated with consistency everyday lead to great achievements gained slowly over time."

- John C. Maxwell

Notes:

DAY 6
Doubt

Rid yourself of **doubt**. Doubt only leads to fear. Whenever doubt enters your mind, you must do your research and look for facts to dismantle it. On this journey, you must take risks. Make sure these are calculated risks. There are two outcomes associated with risks: **victories & lessons**. Once your outcomes are delivered you must take heed of them. Learn from your **LESSONS** and celebrate your **VICTORIES**.

James 1:5-8, "If any of you lack wisdom, let him ask of God, that giveth to all men liberally, and upbraideth not; and it shall be given to him. {6} But let him ask in faith, nothing wavering. For he, that waveth is like a wave of the sea driven with the wind and tossed. {7} For let not that man think that he shall receive anything of the Lord. {8} A double minded man is unstable in all his ways."

To do: Write down the last risk you took. Now write down outcome of this risk and the pros and cons associated with it.

Notes:

DAY 7
Structure

Structure is the foundation that maintains a limitless life journey. You must structure your day, your thoughts, and your emotions. Self-actualization is reaching our full potential and becoming all we are capable of being. Focus on the things in your life that are relevant. Do not spend time wondering if you did well on a test. Instead focus on the outcome and how you can improve. I had a professor that once told me that as long as you study and prepare yourself, the outcome will never be as good as you anticipated it and never as bad as you feared.

Ephesians 5: 15-17, "Look carefully then how you walk, not as unwise but as wise. Making the best use of the time because the days are evil. Therefor do not be foolish but understand what the will of the Lord is.

"Where you see wrong or inequality or injustice; speak out because this is your country. This is your democracy. Make it, Protect it. Pass it on."

- Thurgood Marshall

Notes:

DAY 8
Tribe

There are many factors that help determine a **tribe**. A **tribe** could be a relationship among people that speak the same language, share similar beliefs, and live in the same area. Exploring **tribes** and learning about other cultures will benefit you while on your path to freedom. We often overlook the value in diversity. Diversity introduces compassion, understanding, and ultimately nurturing evolution.

Galatians 3:28: "There is neither Jew nor Gentile, neither slave nor free, nor is there male and female; for you all one Christ Jesus."

"We all have a soul family, the ones that ignite and support our truth. They feed something in us we weren't aware we needed before them. They'll make you face yourself and become raw and authentic. You'll roam but never too far from each other for the invisible thread of connectedness, once opened can never be locked. They are the ones who will see you through all the important days of your life no matter what tributes and trials you face. They'll just be there, in presence, in synchronicity or in spirit."

-Nikki Rowe

To do: I challenge you to reach out to your **tribe** and let them know the significance they play in your life.

Notes:

DAY 9
Tasks

Completing **tasks** gives you a sense of accomplishment. No matter how small or big the **tasks** are, when you complete a task, it will inadvertently give you confidence in taking on new tasks. Completing **tasks** is the ultimate goal. Accidentally nurturing confidence is social security.

Colossians 3:23-24: "Whatever you do, work at it with all your heart, as working for the Lord, not for human masters."

Acts 20:24: "However, I consider my life worth nothing to me; my only aim is to finish the race and complete the task the Lord Jesus has given me the task of testifying to the good news of God's grace."

Notes:

DAY 10
Encourage

Empathetic listening is a structured, non-judgmental communication technique that involves focusing entirely on the speaker's emotional experience and perspective rather than merely hearing their words. I did some action research on one job to see why turnover was so high. Most of the employees did not feel their opinions mattered. Relatedness is the feeling of being connected to others in one's social environment and feeling worthy of love and respect. We came up with suggestion boxes and started having weekly town hall meetings where employees could share their opinions.

You can encourage yourself in a multitude of ways, like daily affirmations; surround yourself with positivity and always remember that you are resilient. Your efforts are beneficial no matter how small.

Hebrew 10:24-25: "And let us consider how we may spur one another on toward love and good deeds, not giving up, meeting together, as some are in the habit of doing. But encouraging one another and all more as you see the Day approaching."

"I think the greatest thing we give each other is encouragement. Knowing that I'm talking to someone in this mentoring relationship who's interested in the big idea here is very, very important to me. I think if

were just about helping me get to the next step, it would be a heck of lot less interesting."

- Anne Sweeny

Notes:

DAY 11
Consistency

Consistency is mandatory to preserve structure. Restore your faith daily. A just man falls down seven times. What makes a man just? A just man walks with integrity and humility and does not show favoritism. If a just man falls seven times and redeems himself seven times, imagine a man that is lost and has no direction. How many times must an unjust man fall and get back up? An **infinite** number of times is the answer. Iteration is the process of repetition to attain a specific goal. The number seven is significant because it is the number of completion.

Proverbs 24:16: "For though the righteous fall seven times, they rise again, but the wicked stumble when calamity strikes."

"Motivation gets you going, but discipline keeps you growing. That is the Law of Consistency."

- John C. Maxwell

Notes:

DAY 12
Time

Time is the most valuable possession that each of us has. What you do with your time will determine if you have a limitless journey in your life. My father always told me that there is a time and a place for everything. He went a little further and expounded on it, saying that when you study/research go hard. When you are on the football field, give it 110%, and when you party, let loose. Time is of the essence. Make your time. Your time is valuable.

Ecclesiastes 3:1: "There is a time for everything and a season for every activity under the heavens."

"In learning you will teach, in teaching you will learn."

- Phil Collins

Notes:

DAY 13
Educate

Educate yourself in every aspect of your life. Empowerment occurs when students gain the ability to apply things they have been taught. Being a part of the education world has allowed me the opportunity to continue my passion for learning. My teaching becomes their doing! When students can practice and apply what they have learned until it becomes a skill, that is empowerment. From our earliest childhood memories, we were taught how to learn. We should begin our journey by educating ourselves. A task that teachers face is the ability to translate that which is being taught into real-world benefits. Teachers are students' first line of resources. Communication is one of the most important pieces of **education**. Teachers who facilitate from an empowerment perspective desire their students to know as much as possible about the subject matter. Students are empowered because they experience encouragement and support from their **educators**. No one can take what you learn away from you.

One motto that I live by is that I teach our youth how to think critically and solve problems, not what to think. I had professor that once told me to always be a part of the solution and never be part of the problem.

Ephesians 6:1-4: "Children, obey your parents in the Lord, for this is right. Honor your father and mother, which is the first commandment with a promise—so that it may go well with you and that you may enjoy long life on the earth. Fathers, do not exasperate your children; instead, bring them up in the training and instruction of the Lord."

"Education is our passport to the future, for tomorrow belongs to the people who prepare for it today."

- Malcolm X

Notes:

DAY 14
Vision

Do not underestimate your **vision.** Your **vision** may not align with your peers. Your **vision** allows you the freedom to see things that may not be capable of being seen by any other person but you. The ability to act to what is unknown will make fear and doubt dissipate. Align your vision with your character and foster the things that shine light to your **vision**.

I had a professor, Dr. Hocutt, that challenged me to align my vision with my character without limitations. I had always considered my circumstances to determine my actions on pursuing my **vision.** Disregard your circumstances. Do not consider salary with your vision, and do not limit yourself to the time and effort you spend on your **vision**. I challenge you to align your vision with your actions.

Numbers 12:6: "And he said, Hear now my words: If there be a prophet among you, I the Lord will make myself known unto him in a vision, and will speak unto him in a dream."

"What happens to a dream deferred? Does it dry up like a raisin in the sun? Or does it explode?"

- Langston Hughes

To do: Create a **vision** board. The bigger the better. Place the things on your **vision** board to which you are innately drawn. Allow yourself the freedom to see things that you may not be able to physically touch.

Notes:

DAY 15
Self-Awareness

The ability to rely on self and sustain self-sufficiency hinges on your **self-awareness**. A good friend of mine taught me a valuable lesson in life about cognition. He taught himself how to speak and write English. He is fluent in seven languages, and he started moving away from his native land at the age of fifteen. He was aware and this gave him the ability to be conscious and disciplined to bind his feelings, emotions, and desires to obtain freedom.

Proverbs 14:23: "A wise man doesn't display his knowledge, but a fool displays his foolishness."

Proverbs 27:17: "As iron sharpens iron, so one person sharpens another."

"You never know how strong you are until being strong is your only choice." - Bob Marley

Notes:

DAY 16
Resilience

Toughness is the first word that comes to mind when we think of **resilience**. Having **resilience** is like when a vehicle is dented and you are able to pop it back into its original position. Being able to recover from difficult circumstances is the true meaning of **resiliency**. One result stemming from recovering from difficult circumstances is we often learn how to adapt. Adapting to difficult circumstances and maintaining integrity guarantees a limitless journey.

Philippians 4:13: "I can do all things through Christ who strengthens me."

"Be like water."

- Bruce Lee

Notes:

DAY 17
Humility

I was humbled early in my life. When you become humbled, you obtain a trait that is truly life changing. Being humble allows you to be teachable. Before I was humbled, it was self-abasement. After I was humbled, everything was made for love. Your perspective will shift from tunnel vision to looking through a kaleidoscope. Your perspective will become clear, sharp, and colorful. We must appreciate all cultures. Instead of just acknowledging different cultures, we must study and embrace (or adopt) the rudiments that are aligned with our purpose.

Proverbs 22:4: "Humility is the fear of the Lord: its wages are riches and honor and life."

"If you look how long the Earth has been here, we're living in the blink of an eye. So, whatever it is your want to do, you go out and do it."

- Jamie Foxx

Notes:

DAY 18
Persistence

Being persistent is not the same as being consistent. **Persistence** encapsulates resistance. Be **persistent** with everything you do that aligns with your purpose. Becoming persistent you will encounter many obstacles. The ability not to be affected by something is called resistance. Having resistance gives you a character trait that helps you reach freedom. I challenge you when times become tough to remain **persistent**.

James 1:12: "Blessed is the one who perseveres under trial because, having stood the test, that person will receive the crown of life that the Lord has promised to those who love him."

Galatians 6:9: "So let's not get tired of doing what is good. At just the right time we will reap a harvest of blessing if we don't give up.

Ephesians 6:12: "For our struggle is not against flesh and blood, but against the rulers, against, the authorities, against the powers of this dark world and against the spiritual forces of evil in the heavenly realms."

"If you succumb to the temptation of using violence in the struggle, unborn generations will be the recipients of long and dissolute night of bitterness."

- Rev. Dr. Martin Luther King, Jr.

Notes:

DAY 19
Restraint

Having **restraint** often gives you a level of self-awareness that many of us seek. **Restraint** is the act of holding back, controlling, or limiting actions, emotions, or freedom, as well as the devices that impose restrictions. Possessing **restraint** does not mean to tolerate injustice or inequality, you must hone that energy to establish a path or trail that demands justice or equality. I had a cousin that was brutally murdered by law enforcement, and he thought that having restraint would allow him justice. **#JUSTICEFORAMOS**

Isaih 1:17: "Learn to do right, seek justice. Defend the oppressed. Take up the cause of the fatherless; plead the case of the widow."

"I realize I will always be the poster child for police brutality, but I can try to use that as a positive force for healing and restraint."

- Rodney King

Notes:

DAY 20
Passion

What are you **passionate** about? What drives you to achieve goals while enduring hardship? For example, bodybuilders are **passionate** about their bodies, so they endure muscle soreness, body fatigue, and extreme dieting. Until age 17 or 18, most of us are **passionate** about pleasing our parents/guardians. Whether you enter into the workforce, scholastic world, or military, you will be tasked with enduring some hardship to attain certain goals. When will you please God? Do not spend your life dedicated to pleasing others. In order to reach a limitless life, you must align your **passions** with your purpose.

Matthew 6:21: "For where your treasure is, there your heart will be also."

"Truth is, everybody is going hurt you, you just gotten find the ones worth suffering for."

- Bob Marley

To do: Write down five things you are **passionate** about. Next, unite these passions with your daily activities.

Notes:

DAY 21
Preparedness

There has always been a debate on how to define success. Roman philosopher, Seneca, said that "Success is when **preparation** meets opportunity." One might ask, what if they do not feel as though he/she has direction or purpose in life. What are you **preparing** for? If you feel that you do not have a purpose, you are not alone. Many of us do not know what we are preparing for.

I challenge you to create your own success. Every day you obtain success. Acknowledge when you complete that assignment, give thanks when you have nutritious meal, and always listen to your elders. By acknowledging that you completed that assignment, you build confidence that encourages completing the next assignment. Giving thanks for your nutritious meal keeps you humble. By listening to your elders, hopefully you will not repeat cycles that have a stronghold on your elders.

Matthew 24:42-44: "Therefor keep watch, because you do not know on what day your Lord will come. But understand this: If the owner of the house had known at what time of night the thief was coming, he would have kept watch and would not have let his house be broken into. So, you also must be ready, because the Son of Man will come at an hour when you do not expect Him."

Notes:

DAY 22
Perspective

Our lives are not depicted by our environment. Be cautious of the things you want vs the things you need to maintain your freedom. Our **perspective** of ourselves should align with our actions. One of our biggest downfalls is relying on other people to set the standard for our living conditions. DO NOT live your life comparing it to your peers, parents, or society. My cousin always tells me that "errythang ain't for errybody." Fear plus motivation equals anxiety. Your path to freedom is designed specifically for you. Have you ever tried reframing? Reframing is taking a tough situation and looking at it from a different **perspective**. Depression and anxiety are two of the most crimpling diseases. Often depression and anxiety are rooted with comparison. You set the standard of living!

---

2 Timothy 1:7: "For God has not us a spirit of fear, but of power and of love and of sound mind."

"I've learned that people will forget what you said, people will forget what you did, and but people will never forget how you made them feel."

- Maya Angelou

Notes:

DAY 23
11:11

There are many references to 11:11. There is significance of spiritual awakening, rapid manifestation of thoughts into reality, and alignment with the universe. I had a college professor that showed me the significance of 11:11. Knowing your purpose will allow you the freedom to live a limitless life. Create an avenue for your mind to transition or evolve. Mental, spiritual, and physical daily restoration. I & I is a spiritual oneness. I love how Rastafarians believe in the unity of the individual and that God is present in every person. One love, one life, and one God.

Isaiah 11:11: "In that day the Lord will put out his hand a second time to bring back His people who are left. He will bring back them back from Assyria, Egypt, Pathros, Cush, Elam, Shinar, Hanath, and from the islands of the sea."

John 10:30: "I and the Father are one."

"Emancipate yourselves from mental slavery. None but ourselves can free our minds."

- Bob Marley

Notes:

DAY 24
Growth

Grow daily. **Growth** will allow your mind to remain free. Whether you are growing into your adolescent hood or adulthood, grow every day. Many of us struggle with the "status quo." The "status quo" is allowing the existing state of our circumstances to be the normal. We must actively pursue new behaviors and attitudes outside of your tribe, while still experiencing the support, encouragement, positive pressure of your tribe.

Deuteronomy 6:6-7: "These commandments that I give your today are to be on your hearts. Impress them on your children. Talk about them when you sit at home and when you walk along the road, when you lie down, and when you get up."

"Travel is fatal to prejudice, bigotry, and narrow-mindedness."

- Mark Twain

Notes:

DAY 25
Value

Place **value** in everything you do, whether it be taking out the trash or washing dishes. Understanding **value** makes everyday decisions far less cumbersome. Prioritize your day with the things that you **value** most. Place **value** in your thoughts, emotions, and actions. Even place **value** in what you read, watch, and listen to. Everything you take in, including books or music, can influence your mood.

---

1 Timothy 4:8: "For while bodily training is of some value, godliness is of value in every way, as it holds promise for the present life and also for the life to come."

Galatians 5:22-23: "But the fruit of the Spirit is love, joy, peace, forbearance, kindness, goodness, faithfulness, gentleness, and self-control."

To do: Write down five things in your life that hold the most **value.**

Notes:

DAY 26
Liberation

We are given three passageways to communicate with God: mind, body, and soul. Our goal is to be **liberated** mentally, physically, and spiritually. We can speak to God anytime and anywhere, we can look how Jesus moved while on Earth, and we are gifted with intuition to know right from wrong. Whenever you feel constrained, ask God to remove those constraints. Many people speak of financial freedom. Your actions must align with your purpose, and your freedom will be everlasting.

John 3:16: "For God so loved the world that he gave his one and only Son, that whoever believes in Him shall not perish but have everlasting life."

Isaiah 1:17: "Whoever oppresses the poor shows contempt for their Maker, but whoever is kind to the needy honors God."

"When I liberate myself, I liberate others. If you do not speak out ain't nobody going to speak out for you."

- Fannie Lou Haner

Notes:

DAY 27
Procrastination

Procrastination is the intentional, habitual, or irrational delay of tasks despite knowing there will be negative consequences. **Procrastination** is something that we have all encountered. It is the brain's core desire to avoid discomfort in favor of a short-term mood. It does not mean laziness. It simply means prolonged due to lack of confidence in self, or doubt.

Matthew 6:34: "Therefore do not worry about tomorrow, for tomorrow will worry about its own things. Sufficient for the day is its own trouble."

Proverbs 10:4: "He who has slack hand becomes poor, But the hand of the diligent makes rich."

"Don't put off until tomorrow what you can do today."

-Benjamin Franklin

Notes:

DAY 28
Initiative

Initiative is the plan that is fostered by your passion and purpose. Think about the number of times you have said something like, "I need to exercise," I need to lose weight, or "I need to go to the store." How do these affirmations influence your motivation? Always speak highly of things that align with your purpose. Today's society offers unlimited technology. When times arise that you do not feel motivated, I challenge you to look at your vision board and remember why it was created.

Lamentations 3:40: "Let us search and try your ways and turn again to the Lord."

Time is neutral and does not change things. With courage and initiative, leaders change things."

- Jesse Jackson

Notes:

DAY 29
Patience

Emotional intelligence is the ability to perceive, understand, and manage emotions in ourselves and others. We are able to perceive and understand emotions in ourselves and others, but we are not equipped to manage emotions of others. Developing **patience** gives you a trait that balances many qualities. Have you have ever been overwhelmed? Develop **patience.** Have you have ever been anxious? Develop **patience.** Have you ever felt alone? Develop **patience.** Have you ever questioned God? **Develop patience.**

Romans 12:12: "Rejoice in our confident hope. Be patient in trouble and keep on praying."

Romans 8:25: "But if we look forward to something we don't yet have, we must wait patiently and confidently."

Romans 12:3: "For by the grace of God given to me I say to everyone of you not to think more highly of himself and of his importance and ability than he ought to think; but think as to have sound judgement, as God has apportioned to each a degree of faith, and purpose designed for service."

"The only way to have a friend is to be one."

- Ralph Waldo Emerson

Notes:

DAY 30
Prayer

My mama has always said that if all else fails, then to try Jesus. **Prayer** is the keystone to communicating with God. The keystone is the part of the arch that locks all other pieces into place, and it is essential for structural integrity. When I was thirteen, I prayed and asked God what is my purpose? God showed me that I am here to take care of my family and help as many people get to Him. While I served in the United States Air Force, my job was a structural engineer. As a structural engineer, integrity is the key ingredient in determining whether a building is designed properly and if you can proceed with breaking ground. **Prayer** is a time when you have uninterrupted communication with God. Grow through what you go through! While you pray, ask for specifics and clarity to give you understanding that you seek.

Acts 4:13: "Now when they saw the boldness of Peter and Joshua, and perceived that they were unlearned and ignorant men, they marveled; and they took knowledge of them, that they had been with Jesus."

"Do not pray for easy lives. Pray to be stronger men. Do not pray for tasks equal to your powers, pray for powers equal to your tasks."

- Phillip Brooks

Notes:

DAY 31
Self-Reflection

Take time every day to review and evaluate your day. Always make today better than yesterday. As you reflect upon your day, release any emotions that are attached to that day. If there are no immediate threats, then allow those emotions to motivate you to prepare for the next day. One thing many of us struggle with is **self-reflection** and accountability to oneself. Place on your vision board to self-reflect daily. Start a journal to express your **self-reflection** and see your growth as you nurture self-improvement.

---

2 Corinthians 13:5: "Examine yourselves, whether ye be in the faith; prove your own selves. Know ye not your own selves, how that Jesus Christ is in you, except ye be reprobates?

"Be yourself: everyone else is already taken."

- Oscar Wilde

Notes:

About the Cover

The cover of this book aligns with every message within its pages. This vision was shown to me in a dream in June 2004. I have always believed that we are all children of God. Every day is an opportunity to learn from yesterday, cease the moment for that day, and prepare for a better tomorrow. By taking up His cross daily, we pour into ourselves the tools and skills that will bring joy tomorrow. We are cultivating our mind to grow more aligned with our purpose.

About the Author

With a career spanning education, leadership, and industry, this author brings a unique blend of real-world experience and classroom expertise to their work. Currently serving as a 6-12 grade Teacher that specialize in career and technical education, equipping students with practical skills in technology, device management, and problem-solving. Beyond the classroom, he is committed to student development—founding after-school programs such as a fitness initiative and chess club, sponsoring student organizations, and providing academic tutoring in math and reading.

He completed a Master of Arts in Teaching from Walden University, building on a Bachelor of Science in Business Administration from Samford University. Their academic background is complemented by hands-on experience across multiple industries, including manufacturing, retail management, and operations leadership.

Prior to returning to education, the author held several leadership roles, including Plant Supervisor, Shift Supervisor, and Team Manager, where he oversaw operations, trained teams, improved safety compliance, and implemented performance-driven systems. HIs early career also includes service as a Structural Craftsman in the United States Air Force Reserve, he they developed discipline, technical expertise, and a strong foundation in teamwork.

Throughout his career, he has demonstrated a passion for mentoring, leadership development, and continuous improvement. Whether managing teams, coaching athletes, or guiding students, his focus remains the same: helping others reach their full potential.

In addition to his professional work, the author has contributed as a published curriculum content writer and has been actively involved in community service, including work as a Court Appointed Special Advocate (CASA) and leadership roles in nonprofit and alumni organizations.

Blending practical experience with a passion for teaching, this author writes with the goal of inspiring growth, resilience, and lifelong learning in every reader.

www.ingramcontent.com/pod-product-compliance
Lightning Source LLC
LaVergne TN
LVHW091248110826
845146LV00001BA/431

9798234098764